P9-DBI-158

CREATIVE
RUBBER STAMPING
TECHNIQUES

CREATIVE
RUBBER
STAMPING
TECHNIQUES

MARYJO MCGRAW

NORTH LIGHT BOOKS
Cincinnati, Ohio

ABOUT THE AUTHOR

MaryJo McGraw is a nationally known rubber stamp artist whose work has been featured in leading rubber stamp publications. She has taught rubber stamp classes for ten years at stamp stores around the country and has conducted demonstrations and classes at all the major national retail stamp shows. She has been a sample artist for many of the largest stamp manufacturers and has sold her artwork to several art stamp companies.

Her original ideas and techniques and innovative use of materials make her a much sought after stamping instructor for demonstrations and classes.

Creative Rubber Stamping Techniques. Copyright © 1998 by MaryJo McGraw. Manufactured in China. All rights reserved. No part of this book may be reproduced in any form or by any electronic or mechanical means including information storage and retrieval systems without permission in writing from the publisher, except by a reviewer, who may quote brief passages in a review. Published by North Light Books, an imprint of F&W Publications, Inc., 1507 Dana Avenue, Cincinnati, Ohio 45207. (800) 289-0963. First edition.

Other fine North Light Books are available from your local bookstore, art supply store or direct from the publisher.

02 01 00 99 98   5 4 3 2 1

Library of Congress Cataloging-in-Publication Data

McGraw, MaryJo.
   Creative rubber stamping techniques / by MaryJo McGraw.
     p.   cm.
  Includes index.
  ISBN 0-89134-878-6 (pbk. : alk. paper)
  1. Rubber stamp printing. I. Title.
TT867.M3497 1998
761—dc21   98-14960
                                        CIP

Edited by Greg Albert and Jane Friedman
Production edited by Amanda Magoto
Interior designed by Mary Barnes Clark
Cover designed by Stephanie Redman
Cover photography by Guildhaus Photographics

A huge thank you to a few friends and family who keep me inspired by creating beautiful objects of art from the humble rubber stamp. Thanks to Karen Morikawa, Christy Erickson and P.J. Dutton—the ladies who keep me on my toes with ideas, gorgeous cards and encouragement. From these three I look forward to the question "I wonder what would happen if . . . ?" Thanks to my dear friends Hank and Shirley Hardee for just being there for me every day, and to Lea Everse, Diane Lewis, Frankie Fioretti, Kat Okamoto, Teesha and Tracy Moore and Mike and Chris Meador—you are the people I envy for your endless ability to amaze and inspire us all with your art. And the biggest thanks to my parents, Ray and Dorothy Uvaas, for never holding me back.

Table of Contents

Beyond stamps and ink . . . what
you'll need to complete out-of-the-
ordinary projects, how to ink and
clean your stamps, and an image
library of diverse stamps to own.

So you're hooked on embossing?
Wait until you layer embossing
powders—you'll create exciting
textures that range from smooth
enamel to cobblestone.

Take super embossing one step fur-
ther and give a highly unusual look
to your pieces. Make your greeting
cards look like molded metal or
carved stone.

INTRODUCTION

Making Greeting Cards With Rubber Stamps explored many of the basic techniques rubber stampers frequently use. However, stampers are in no way limited to those methods. The exploration of creative ideas for rubber stamps will allow you to create more artistic greetings with rubber stamps and accessories.

Some of the most intriguing techniques involve everyday rubber stamping accessories, such as embossing powders, metallic pens, poly and paper clays, unusual papers, paper cords, sealing wax, ribbons, beads, tassels and even household items like bleach. Trying things you never thought of before is the main idea. As you become more adventurous, try these ideas in different combinations. Mix the techniques on each card you do—after all, it's only paper. Creativity should be your goal, not just creating a beautiful card.

To those who do not want to take that big of a step, start small. After a bit of practice, most of the cards in this book will be simple to create. Create a few parts for cards instead of trying to finish a whole card in one sitting.

More Than the Basics

Of course, the basic necessity in rubber stamping is stamps! In the back of this book, you'll find a listing of rubber stamp companies. They can provide you with stamps and most of the supplies.

For the projects presented in this book, however, you'll need more than stamps. Thermographic embossing powders, metallic pens, vellum and sealing wax are a must. Many projects also use poly clays, tassels and beads.

The cards featured in this book can be done in a variety of ways, so don't feel as if you have to purchase specific products to create any given project. The purpose of the examples is to use different techniques to spark your creativity.

Materials

RUBBER STAMPS

I advise buying good quality stamps. There are generally three parts to a stamp—the mount, the cushion and the die. Quality mounts are made from hardwood. The cushion is made of foam that is from ⅛" (32mm) to ¼" (64mm) thick. The die, the most important part of the stamp because it transfers the design, should be closely trimmed.

PAPER

Paper is another main ingredient in rubber stamping. Most of these projects require high-grade card stock to produce beautiful greeting cards. Don't skimp on paper—it will show. One of the papers you need to find is translucent vellum. Be sure it is translucent, as there are many types of vellum, and most are not see-through by any means.

INKS

Dye-based, pigment and permanent inks are all used to achieve specific effects and results. Remember that dyes and solvents dry quickly; pigment inks dry by absorbing through the surface. You'll definitely want black ink in all three forms and a good selection of colors in most inks.

EMBOSSING POWDERS

Thermographic embossing powders are required for many of the cards in this book. Be sure to have a variety of colors; these techniques look great in almost any color. I list my absolute favorites in the back of the book. At this time there are also several size grades of powder available—detail, fine and double-thick are the most common. Detail is an extremely fine ground powder, but because it is so finely ground, it does not raise as much as the other powders. Detail is perfect for very detailed line images. For most of the techniques in this book, I prefer to use fine or double-thick powders because the focus is on adding height.

PENS AND MARKERS

Metallic pens come in many varieties. In chapter seven we will be using water-based and oil-based paint markers. The water-based markers I use are metallic, but they are also available in opaque colors. The oil-based paint pens used in this book are the type you find in stationery stores. Some are felt tip; some are ball point. A good stamp store will carry both.

BRAYERS

Brayers come in such diversity it is hard to choose which kinds to invest in. For my money, the best all-around brayer is a detachable 4" (10.2cm) soft rubber brayer. It will handle most of the jobs you will require of it. Being detachable, it is easy to clean. There are also sponge, acrylic, hard rubber and wood brayers; each one yields a different result.

CLAY

Poly clays (synthetic clays) are fun and very easy to work with. Simply impress stamps into the clay and bake. These pieces make great accents to your greeting cards. Poly clays are carried at most craft stores and some stamp stores, and come in a huge color assortment. I prefer white so I can color it myself.

Paper clays, or papier maché, are simple to use and can air dry, making them very convenient for folks who don't want to invest in drying equipment for poly clays. They are very lightweight, which makes them perfect for jewelry items.

TASSELS AND CORDS

Tassels make a great addition to a beautiful card. The ones used in this book are available at many stamp stores, along with paper cords. These cords can be used in many ways, from decorative purposes to functional applications, such as book binding. Both tassels and cords are typically sold in assorted packs.

WAX

Sealing wax is a cherished accent to envelopes, cards and documents. Now available in a new form—like JudiKins wax wafers—and old-fashioned sticks, wax has taken on new popularity in card making. Also, new sealers are more convenient to use and are updated to use with your stamped cards.

BEADS

Glass beads are a fun embellishment. The ones used here are without holes and with a metal finish, which makes them a natural for paper arts.

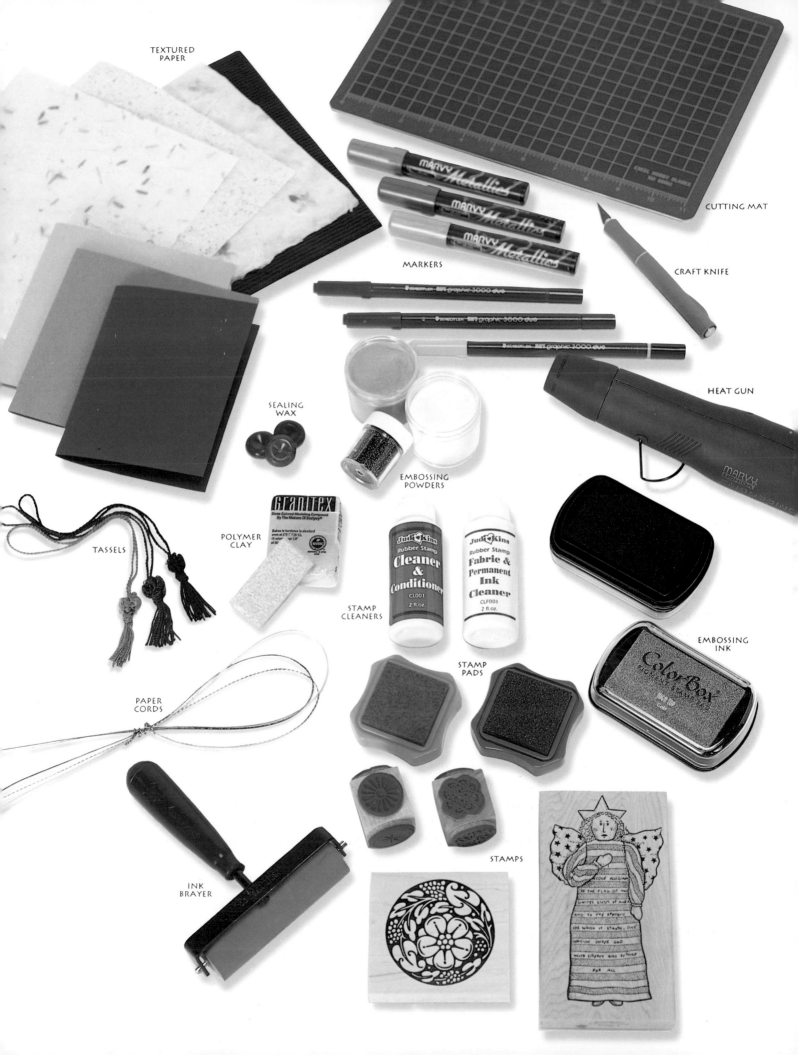

TEXTURED PAPER

CUTTING MAT

MARKERS

CRAFT KNIFE

HEAT GUN

SEALING WAX

EMBOSSING POWDERS

TASSELS

POLYMER CLAY

STAMP CLEANERS

EMBOSSING INK

PAPER CORDS

STAMP PADS

INK BRAYER

STAMPS

Image Library

Since we will be focusing on techniques that require different images, I would like to show you some stamps that work well with these techniques. You'll be able to find most of these images at your local stamp store; if not, the store can help you locate the designs or similar images.

GRAPHIC

Graphic stamps make a bold statement. Often these designs are solid and confident. They can be simple additions to a complex background. Try stamping them in mixed colors for a change of pace. With your fingers, apply different colored pigment inks and blend them directly on the stamp. Stamp onto un-coated stock.

BORDERS

Border stamps can measure from 1" (2.5cm) to 6" (15.2cm) or 7" (17.8cm) in length. I prefer the longest designs because they are simpler to line up as a border. Although most folks use these stamps for creating borders, they also work well for paper weaving, stripes and layered elements. You can create interesting sunburst backgrounds by stamping borders in a circular pattern.

NATURE

Nature images are perfect for seasonal as well as all-occasion cards. Designs of nature's simple pleasures—rocks, animals, shells, large trees and especially leaves—are wonderful additions to any stamp collection. They are common objects that are easily recognizable to many people. You'll never have to answer the question, "What is it?"

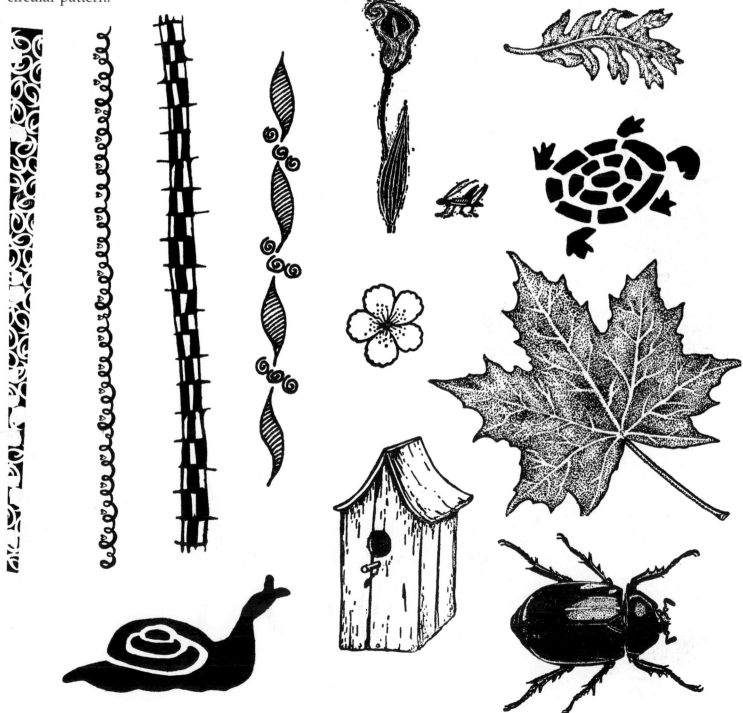

WHIMSICAL

Have you ever seen an image that made you smile immediately? Those stamps fall into this category—designs that please you, that are fun and fanciful, not too cute, yet humorous. These stamps make you want to create cheerful projects. Words can also be included here. Inspirational sayings in fun fonts can sometimes become the theme for a whimsical card.

ELEGANT

These stamps will provide a primary image appropriate for many occasions. The designs are great for greeting cards and work well for many techniques, especially embossing. Other images that could fall into this category include floral, art deco and art nouveau. When searching for elegant images, look for crisp designs that would be useful for an all-occasion card.

CULTURAL

Asian, Mayan, Celtic and African are just a few of the cultural stamps available. Some of the designs that are now rubber stamps started out as fabric printing blocks in these cultures, meaning they are great for fabric and textured papers. Some of the designs have specific meanings, and several of the stamp companies put these meanings on the sides of the stamps or in their catalogs.

WAX SEALS

These stamps are made specifically for use with sealing waxes and super embossing techniques. They also work on paper and some fabrics. The designs are usually in the negative so that the wax will rise up into the stamp and create the image. These particular stamps are made from a harder rubber compound, making them easier to use on melted wax or embossing powders.

Basic Inking and Cleaning

INK YOUR STAMP WITH A DYE-BASED PAD

Now that we've covered the materials, we can move on to the basic techniques of inking and cleaning your stamps.

1 Tap the stamp several times on the dye-based pad.

2 Check the rubber side to see that the raised portion is completely covered with the ink. If it is, stamp it on some scrap paper. How does it look? Did you pick up the edges from the untrimmed parts of the stamp? If you did, you probably used too much pressure. Try again. Stamp it again and again until you get a good feel for it. Now re-ink the stamp and try it on card stock.

INK YOUR STAMP WITH A WATER-BASED MARKER

If you're just starting out, try using your water-based markers directly on the rubber die. Just color specific areas with different color markers and stamp it. Warm it by breathing on it and stamp it again. You can usually get several impressions with one inking.

Cleaning Your Stamp

You'll need to clean the stamp before you use a different color. You can clean stamps with water or with a soap solution of half cleaner and half water. Most stamp companies have cleaners available with a scrub top, which is very handy. Cleaning solutions won't damage your stamps: The most damaging thing to your stamps is sunlight. I have had some stamps for fifteen years and haven't lost a single one to cleaning solutions, bleach, paint or solvent inks, so don't be afraid to try new things on your stamps.

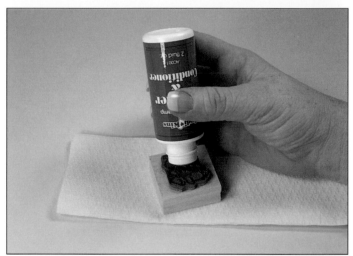

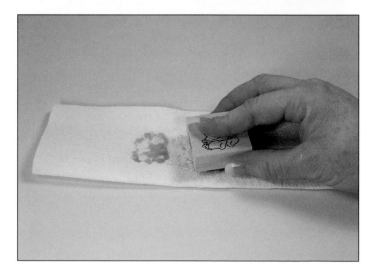

Super Embossing

Most rubber stampers first get hooked on stamping with thermographic embossing: It makes even the simplest design elegant. But once you get past that initial contact with the technique of embossing, what else can be done with it? More than you could imagine.

By layering embossing powders you can create an amazing variety of beautiful looks for your greeting cards. You can begin with a layer that has a cobblestone texture and add a layer to make it smoother. This method can lead you to anything from a rough exterior to a beautiful enamel-like piece of jewelry. So pull out all of your powders, embossing fluid, pigment inks, the heat gun and some paper, make sure you have good ventilation, and get ready for some creative stamping fun.

What You'll Need

THERMOGRAPHIC EMBOSSING POWDERS

There are so many types and colors of powders you'll have trouble choosing among them, but at least have these basics: clear (a double-thick powder like JudiKins Amazing Glaze is perfect), gold, silver and copper. Most stampers also have colors they thought they would like but didn't. Get those old colors out too, because they are perfect to use with this technique.

Before you begin, open all the powders; have several 8½" × 11" (21.6cm × 27.9cm) sheets of scrap paper available to pour the excess powders onto. Many stampers keep powders in small plastic containers for easy access.

EMBOSSING FLUID OR INK

Clear fluid is best for certain techniques, but any type of pigment ink will also work. Keep in mind that the colors will show through on clear-based powders.

A GOOD-QUALITY HEAT GUN

The gun you use is going to be on for quite a while, so it has to hold up. This is also a good time to look into a heat gun holder, like the metal one I use, so you have a safe place to leave it while it is turned on.

CARD STOCK

Start with 5" × 5" (12.7cm × 12.7cm) stock or smaller. Any color will work, but in the beginning choose a paper that doesn't have too much texture. I like colored papers, but white will also work, especially if you stamp the area.

RUBBER STAMPS

Background or graphic stamps work best because bold designs hold up under the powders.

Basic Super Embossing

1 After you stamp your images using a dye ink and have given the ink a minute to dry, apply the embossing fluid to the paper right over the stamped images. This can be done in many different ways. You can apply it by rubbing a pad (either an embossing pad or a light-colored pigment pad) directly on the card, or you can use a brayer to apply the ink. I use a scrub-top container of embossing fluid. This enables me to apply it directly without using any other tool. The scrub top also keeps my pads from picking up ink off the card.

2 Once the paper is covered with ink or fluid, pour on a layer of clear powder.

3 Shake off the excess powder.

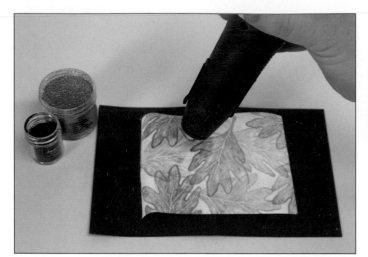

4 Melt the powder with your heat gun. Keeping your heat gun on during this process is crucial: Consistent heat is the key to not scorching the powder or the paper. Try to keep the heat gun low, close to the paper, and move the gun around the paper in a circular motion.

5 When the powder is melted, pour on another layer of the same powder and heat it. This is tricky! It is very important to note that you do not need to add more embossing fluid. After the first layer is sealed and cooled, the embossing fluid will build up and, because it has nowhere to go, will remain floating to the top of your work, leaving a greasy residue. You may always add pigment inks between layers—but not clear embossing fluid. If you stop at this point, the card stock will have a glassy look. If the powder is not thoroughly heated, it will look a bit bumpy, like an orange peel or cobblestone. If you like this look, stop and begin another piece. If you would like to continue, go to the next steps.

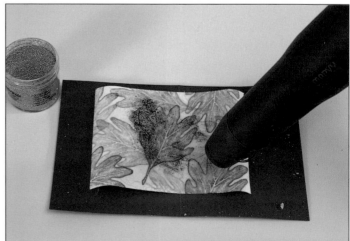

6 Reheat the piece, and then sprinkle on Aegean Silver and Galaxy powders.

7 Reheat. One of the reasons this technique is so satisfying is that you can stop at any time. Trust your instincts—when you feel a piece is complete, stop.

Cracking

Cracking will occur on some of the pieces that you layer. It depends on the number of layers you apply. With one or two layers, cracking is not a big issue; three to five layers constitute prime cracking territory; more than six layers and the chances of cracking lessen because you get a thicker piece.

I don't find cracking to be a big problem. Simply reheat the powder to reseal the crevice, or apply a contrasting ink to the crevices to accentuate the cracks, and then reheat. **Hint**: Be sure to apply the finished part to your card while the surface is still warm and pliable. This prevents the possibility of you cracking it yourself. And remember, mailing anything that is of a ¼" (6mm) or more in thickness requires extra postage.

Recipes

Here are a few super embossing recipes to try.

RECIPE ONE

Stamp white paper with plum and bright yellow dye-based inks. Let dry. Spread embossing fluid over entire piece. Pour on Amazing Glaze and heat. When hot, pour on a second layer of powder, and then sprinkle with Garnet and Egyptian Gold powders. Finish with another layer of glaze.

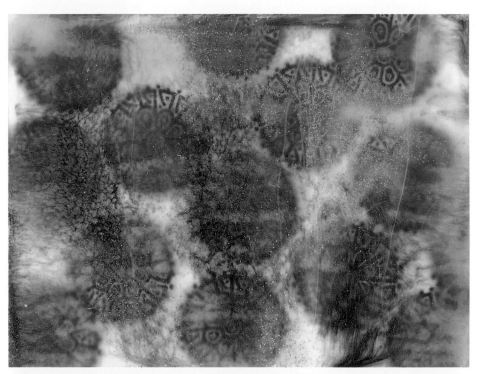

RECIPE TWO

Stain white paper with bright blue dye-based ink. Stamp the sun in red dye-based ink. Spread embossing fluid over the piece. Use two layers of Amazing Glaze. Sprinkle on Aegean Silver and Jasper powders. While hot, swirl with a chopstick. Stamp the sun on top of the cooled layer with gold pigment-based ink, and then emboss with translucent gold.

RECIPE THREE

Stamp feather in light green, dark green and lavender. Cover with embossing fluid. Pour on Kaleidoscope powder. Heat and add one layer of Amazing Glaze, and then add one layer of white powder. While hot, scrape with a chopstick. Add a final layer of glaze.

RECIPE FOUR

Stamp heart on white paper with gold pigment-based ink and emboss in Garnet powder. Color in the hearts with yellow and pine green pens. Brayer on embossing fluid. Add two layers of Amazing Glaze.

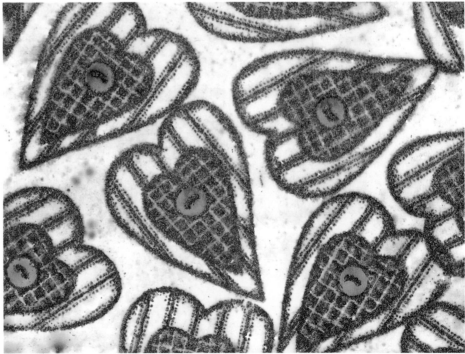

Flute Player

1 Begin by stamping the flute player and the large music sheet in black dye-based ink on a large piece of uncoated white card stock. Using a cosmetic sponge, apply yellow dye-based ink to the images. On the music sheet, use a random application; on the flute player, apply it over the entire piece. Cut the music sheet into a square at least 3½″ × 3½″ (8.9cm × 8.9cm). Around the flute player, cut an uneven-edge rectangle. At this point, sponge on a rust color dye-based ink, working in from the edge of the paper and leaving some of the pure yellow showing through the center. On the music sheet, sponge the same color more evenly across the piece.

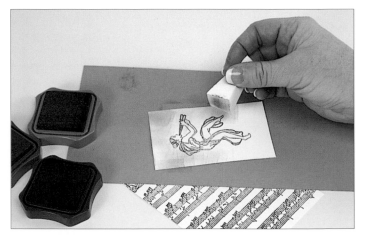

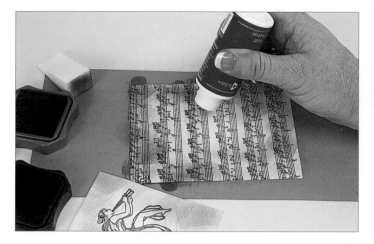

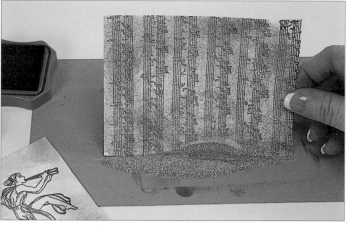

2 Apply embossing fluid to both parts. Cover the music sheet with Kaleidoscope powder, shake off the excess and then heat.

3 While the piece is hot, immediately pour on Amazing Glaze powder. Pour off the excess and heat again until the powder is thoroughly melted. Set this part aside to cool. Pour Amazing Glaze onto the flute player piece, heat it and then repeat the process.

4 I put this card together with double-stick tape. Start with a square tan card layer on the music background. Layer the flute player onto a piece of purple cardstock, leaving a bit of a border all around. Add this part to the music sheet.

Relic Background Card

1 On this card I took a super-embossed scrap that I made from a sage green notecard. I like using the torn edge as an element in cards; keeping the other three sides even makes it easy to affix this piece to another card of the same size. Embossing the scrap with Lapis Lazuli, Translucent Gold and Amazing Glaze gives the piece an enamel look. After the piece cooled, I folded it in a square pattern.

2 Folding allows you to achieve some wonderful cracks. I dabbed a bit of blue pigment-based ink on the cracks.

3 I coated the blue ink with Lapis Lazuli powder and heated it.

4 The cracks reseal, but leave a great texture on the paper. At this point I added gold squiggles to the light blue card with gold embossing powder, and then attached the enamel-looking part.

5 The final embossed element is added. Once you have the basics down, the possibilities are endless, as you can see in the next two pages.

Endless Possibilities

Add glass beads between layers. Mix melted waxes in. Use tinsel or paper cords. Try a piece of a doily or a scrap of stamped paper. Incorporate sea shells or silk leaves. Use real leaves dipped in clear embossing fluid. Squiggle metallic pens on cooled pieces. Use old game parts, puzzle pieces and postage stamps.

(top) Textured Treasure: *Super emboss Dk green cardstock with Amazing Glaze. Set aside for a day then reheat the piece. The embossed piece will become very textured. Stamp and emboss a solid image on tan cardstock, and while hot, sprinkle on glaze. Rim each part with a copper paint pen, and layer as shown.*

(right) Copper Heart: *Super emboss a large heart stamp in copper. While the piece is still hot, scrape away some of the melted powder with a craft knife. Apply the heart to a stamped piece. Layer onto a square notecard.*

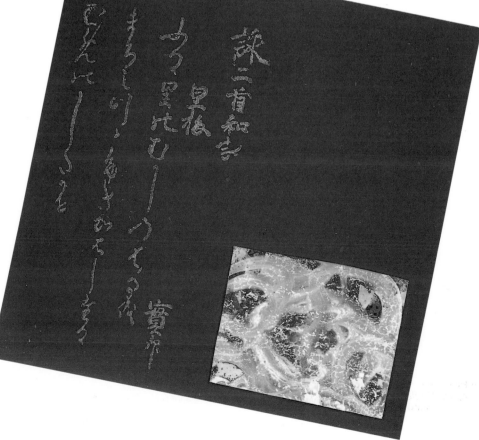

(top left) **Water-Washed Card:**
*Brayer lightly with watercolor on
two pieces of light-colored cardstock. Emboss in clear powder a
large stamp on the background
layer. Repeat that step with a
smaller stamp for the top layer.
Speckle the top piece with a toothbrush dipped in silver paint.*

(top right) **Golden Relic:** *Super
emboss a piece of black matte cardstock with gold and clear powders, then stamp three images on
top of the piece in a multicolored
powder. Tear the edges so the
piece can lay at a slight angle
across a notecard. Emboss the
same images in clear on the
notecard.*

(bottom) **Trip to Japan:** *Cut a
small square of super embossed
paper. Glue to the corner of an
uncoated notecard. Stamp a design in gold pigment ink.*

Embedded Stamps

This technique builds on what you learned in the first chapter: Using it can give an unusual look to greeting cards. Pieces can look like molded metal or carved stone. By layering embossing powders to higher levels, you can create a pool of melted powder in which you embed your stamp.

The first question I am *always* asked after someone sees me do this technique is "Doesn't that hurt the rubber?" The answer is a resounding *"No!"* Most rubber is vulcanized at over 400°F (204°C), so this bit of heated powder can do no harm. Remember: Nothing will hurt the rubber die part of the stamp except constant exposure to sunlight. As long as you wipe off the rubber with a good stamp cleaner or water, you can even use solvents or straight bleach on your stamps. This particular method is a bit tricky in the beginning, but with a little practice you'll embed your stamps with ease.

Verdigris Dog

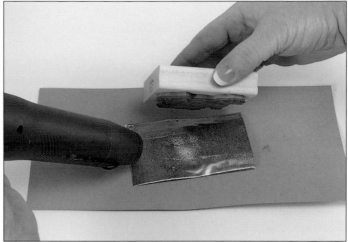

1 Here is an easy beginning card for first-time embedding. Start with a 3″×4″ (7.6cm×10.2cm) piece of purple card stock. Have your rubber stamp within easy reach. Cover the stock with embossing fluid or purple pigment-based ink. Pour on Malachite embossing powder and heat.

2 When the powder is hot, pour on another layer; repeat this step. Have your stamp in hand so that you are ready for the next step.

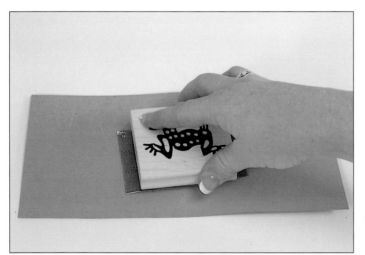

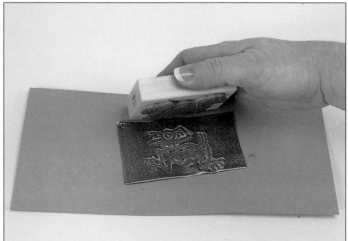

3 Stamp into the hot melted powder. Let the stamp sit in the mixture until the melted powder has hardened, about thirty seconds.

4 Starting at one end, slowly pull out the stamp with a rolling motion. That's it! **Hint**: If the embossing sticks to the stamp, the mixture was too hot. Don't panic—pull off the excess material on your stamp, put it back on the card and reheat it with your heat gun. Add a bit more powder, reheat and try again.

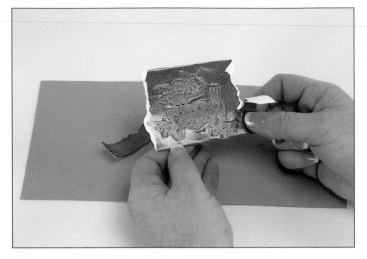

5 At this point in the process, I tore the edges of the card toward me to reveal the rough edge.

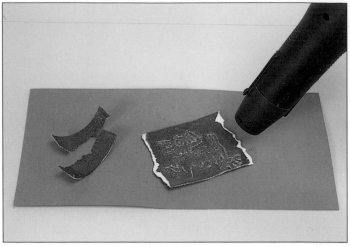

6 Heat the edges to reseal the embossing. You could also color this edge with a metallic pen.

7 I layered this piece to a deckle-edge postcard, embedded it in the same fashion with clear powder instead of a colored one, and then embedded a large squiggle stamp into the clear layer. This look is very subtle: The indentations into the clear layer are not as visible from every angle.

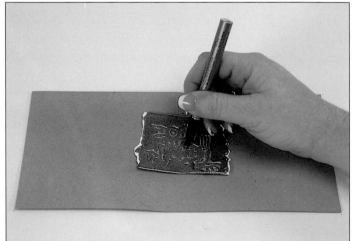

8 After the two parts had set, I took a copper paint marker and accented within the lines of the dog. I repeated the process on the clear-coated part within the lines of the squiggle stamp.

Impress a Big Border

As you can see, bold stamps work well with this technique. On this card I used a large border stamp that has the perfect graphic look. This border has the appearance of metal because of the powders used. You can achieve a similar look with almost any metallic powders.

Begin by using embossing fluid and a colored powder as a base on a 4″ × 7″ (10.2cm × 17.8cm) border strip. Here I used three layers of Jasper, which has a terra cotta look. On top of the Jasper I applied a layer of Translucent Gold powder to give it a burnished appearance.

When the powder is hot, press in the stamp. Let it cool slightly, and pull out the stamp slowly. Now, while the strip is still warm, cut it to the exact size you want with a craft knife. Sometimes after you cut the piece, you'll need to heat the cut edges to reseal them. Apply the finished strip to your card.

Hint: When you are embedding large stamps, you need more layers. A 1″ × 1″ (2.5cm × 2.5cm) rubber stamp needs only one or two layers of embossing powder, but a stamp of the size shown needs at least four layers. Remember: Keep your heat gun low and move it slowly around the piece you are working on, evenly heating the whole piece.

Quick Little Impression

For this fast little number, start with a torn 2″ × 2″ (5.1cm × 5.1cm) square that you have super embossed twice using orange, green and purple pigment-based inks. Let that cool completely, and then crack the piece. Dab in black pigment-based ink in the cracks and emboss with Galaxy powder.

1 With a cosmetic sponge, apply a thick square of gold pigment-based ink.

2 Emboss two layers of Galaxy powder.

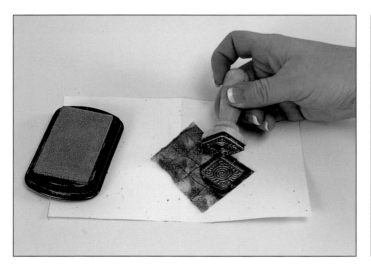

3 Apply the same gold ink to a small stamp and impress it into the melted powder. Embed a small stamp.

4 Apply this finished square to the bottom-right corner of your notecard.

More Embedding Ideas

(top) **Malachite Man:** *Begin with a purple pigment ink as the base for several layers of Amazing Glaze. Add two layers of Malachite powder. While hot, embed the face. Carefully tear the edges while still warm, and layer onto contrasting papers.*

(right) **Celtic Bronze:** *Emboss two layers of Amazing Glaze and one layer of Bronze powder. While hot, embed the stamp into the mixture. Let cool completely. Layer the piece onto stamped and embossed backgrounds.*

(top right) Verdigris Kimono: *Using water-based metallic markers, create a verdigris combination over clay-colored cardstock. Stamp the kimono in black dye ink, and emboss two layers of Amazing Glaze over the piece. Cut out the kimono. Create a textured border strip by embossing layers of Malachite and copper powders. While hot, stamp the mixture with a scrunch stamp.*

(middle left) Here Comes the Sun: *Layer alternating powders (two of each color) on cardstock—in this case, Amazing Glaze and Jasper. Then embed the sun stamp that is covered in gold pigment ink.*

(bottom right) Foil Look: *Let three layers of Amazing Glaze cool. Add random lines of water-based metallic pen over the glaze. Reheat and add another layer of glaze. Embed a cube stamp coated with green pigment ink into the glaze. Reheat lightly to bring back the shine.*

CHAPTER 4

Vellum Techniques

Some of the most fun I've had in stamping has been playing with translucent vellum. It has so many possible looks—from pretty to cute to country to ethnic—and is the perfect paper for all these styles and more. It can look soft and sweet or exotic, depending on technique and color choices.

Some of the simplest stamping ideas are perfect for vellum. Just randomly stamping it on both sides with complementary colors is the perfect overlay for a plain white card.

Vellum is very easy to overdo, especially with embossing: Keep this in mind when working with this particular paper.

A Simple Vellum Card

1 Here's an easy vellum card to start with. Stamp a random pattern on both sides of a 6″ × 11½″ (15.2cm × 29.2cm) piece of vellum with several different colors of dye-based inks. Set this piece aside to dry.

2 Take a square white notecard and stamp a similar pattern on the front using the same colors of inks. Once both parts are completely dry, score the vellum and fold it in half. Run a fine bead of glue on the back of the notecard near the crease.

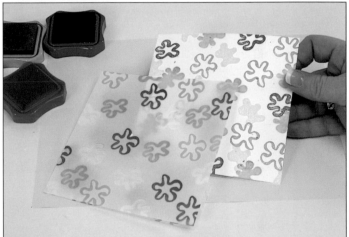

3 Attach the stamped vellum to the notecard.

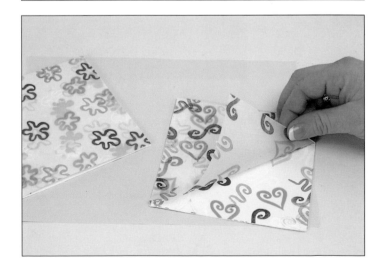

Lady Liberty Card

This is a lovely use for vellum. Try it with elegant or
whimsical images.

1 On a piece of 4″ × 6″ (10.2cm × 15.2cm) vellum, stamp the liberty doll stamp in white pigment-based ink; emboss with white powder.

2 Turn the vellum over, and color the image in on the back of the piece with water-based markers.

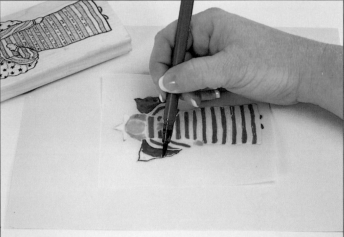

3 Attach the part by tying it on with a simple paper cord: Punch two small holes in the notecard and two more holes in the vellum; thread the paper cord through and knot it.

Techniques to Try

Now let's practice a few other techniques on small (4″ × 6″ [10.2cm × 15.2cm]) pieces of a medium weight (not too heavy) translucent vellum.

EXAMPLE ONE

Take a light-colored raised dye stamp pad, and rub it over one side of the vellum. Let dry completely, or blot well on newsprint. On the other side of the paper, use a slightly deeper color pad, or stamp a few images in that deeper color.

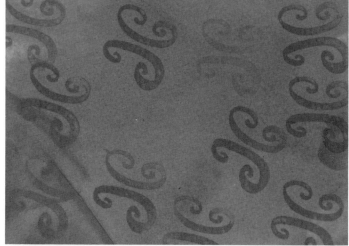

EXAMPLE TWO

On another piece of vellum, stain one side with a deep color and let it dry. With a spritzer bottle, spray a little water over the paper. Small spots will appear, creating a speckled effect. **Note**: The paper will curl when wet. To flatten it, wait until the vellum is almost dry, and then place it under a heavy book.

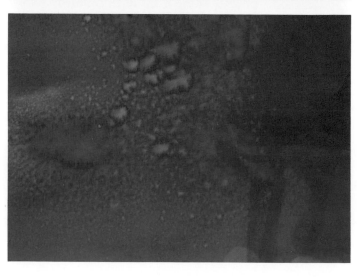

EXAMPLE THREE

On a clean piece, try this technique. Stamp an asymmetrical image on one side of the vellum. When that is dry, turn the paper over and, with the same stamp, stamp in the empty space. This is the perfect technique when you want to have a stamp of a person or animal facing itself.

EXAMPLE FOUR

For a different look, take a stiff-bristle paintbrush, fan brush or stencil brush and swipe color across the vellum. Utilizing several coordinating colors gives an interesting effect. If you don't have a paintbrush, try a toothbrush for speckling, or twist the dye pad to change the look.

EXAMPLE FIVE

Try using metallic water-based markers in brief strokes, or use the markers on a background stamp. Remember: You don't want to lose the translucent quality of the vellum, so this particular technique needs a light touch.

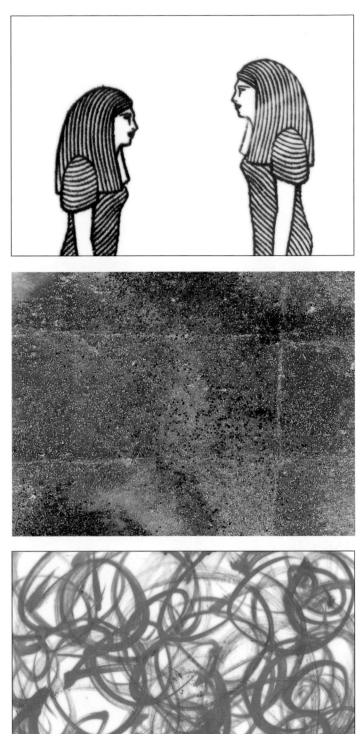

Clear Embossing

1 A fun technique to try is clear embossing on the paper. Using your clear pad and clear powder, emboss a few images all over the vellum.

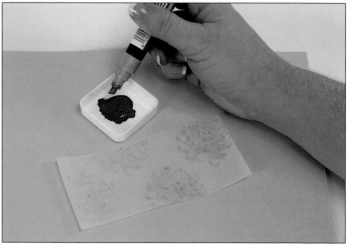

2 When that is cool, spread metallic marker on a paint tray.

3 Using a fan brush, stroke the color over the images.

4 Be sure to blot this well!

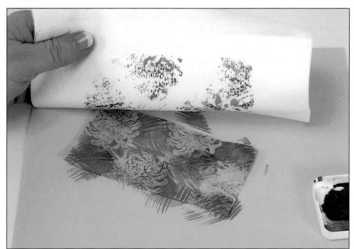

5 Attach the vellum to the front of your card with small pieces of double-stick tape and add a tassel.

Simple Squares

Begin with two 3½″ × 3½″ (8.9cm × 8.9cm) squares of
vellum. Stain one square with a light blue dye-based
ink; stain the other in a light aqua tone. Stamp a large
background stamp in dark blue on the first square;
set aside. Stamp the aqua square with the same stamp
in a turquoise. When the blue square is dry, stamp it
with the same stamp in violet on the opposite side.
Finish the card by lightly gluing the vellum to the
card at an angle. Use a small hole punch to add two
holes about 1″ (2.5cm) from the outside edge. Add a
tassel (or two) through each hole.

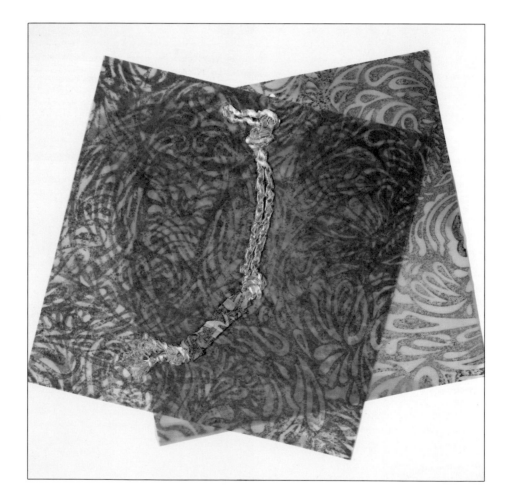

More Vellum Ideas

(top left) **Vellum Strips:** Use stained and stamped leftover strips to collage on cardstock with paper cords.

(middle right) **Paisley Vellum:** On lightweight translucent vellum, rub the surface with light blue dye ink. Let dry. Stamp the same piece of vellum with a large background stamp. Cut a rectangle approximately 4" × 2½" (10cm × 6.5cm), then layer a torn strip of the remaining vellum on top. Trim as needed and apply to a square notecard.

(bottom left) **Ancient Vellum:** Stain a 4" × 4" (10cm × 10cm) square of vellum with an ochre-colored dye pad. Add a light coating of ivory pigment ink, and sprinkle on Malachite powder. While warm, stamp with an Asian seal stamp.

CHAPTER 5

Elegant Embellishments

Sealing wax is no longer just an old-fashioned way to close the back of an envelope or seal a document. It can be a fresh new element on a wedding card or a birthday greeting. In this chapter we'll look at elegant and easy techniques to embellish your cards with new sealing waxes and seals, glass beads, ribbon, tassels and paper cords. You'll uncover new ways to look at old ideas. Many times we look at a card and think, "This needs something, but what?" These elegant embellishments might be just what you've been looking for.

Sealing Wax Basics

STICK WAX

Whether you choose sticks or wafers, there are a few things you need to know. With sticks you need some type of flame to melt the wax. I prefer a barbecue lighter or a small torch to an alcohol lamp. These lighters are safer than regular lighters because they can't burn your hands. Alcohol lamps are fine for doing several applications of wax, but these small units are handy and quicker for one or two applications. When you do use a flame, keep the wax in the blue part of the flame. You'll have less chance of burning the wax, which can leave soot all over your seal.

Hint: When using stick wax, wait at least thirty seconds before putting the seal into the wax. The seal will be much easier to remove from the wax.

WAX WAFERS

Wafers are really the way to go. If you own a heat gun, you'll find them very easy to use. Simply place your wafer where you want it, and warm it with your heat gun. Wafers do not need to be as thoroughly heated as stick wax because you are not trying to move the wax by melting it.

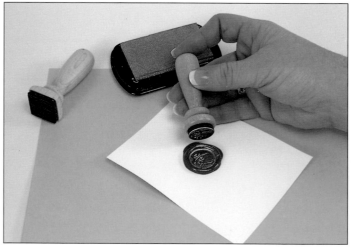

Ink your sealer with pigment-based ink. This will help release the sealer from the wax. If you don't want any color, use clear embossing ink.

Hint: You do not want the wafer falling off your card, so adhere it to the paper well. Scratch the paper with a craft knife where you want it to stick, and then apply the wax. This gives the wax more to hang on to and lessens the chance of it coming off your card.

You can cut a small *x* with your knife and pull up two prongs if you are going to layer the piece on another card. **Hint**: If the sealer is sticking in the wax, be patient: Your wax is probably still too hot. Wait one minute before trying to pull the sealer out again.

The Simple Seal

Begin by stamping a 4″×4″ (10.2cm×10.2cm) piece of sage green card stock with a pattern. I used a large background stamp in reddish dye-based ink and a cube stamp of stars in gold. Attach this part to a square deep blue greeting card. Stamp another image on the sage paper in red, cut it out and layer that onto a piece of the deep blue paper, leaving about an ⅛″ (3mm) border all around. Attach this to the card on the upper left-hand side with double-stick tape. Choose a piece of ribbon as an accent. I chose a dusky green silk ribbon and applied it to the card with a small chip of wax that I heated with my heat gun. When you have the ribbon positioned, lay a wax wafer on it. Heat the wafer until it is soft—but not runny—and press in a sealer.

Combining Ideas

Using what you learned in the first chapter, create a 4″×4″ (10.2cm×10.2cm) square of embossed paper. Here I used several metallic pens for color under Egyptian Gold and clear powders. Cut a strip of corrugated board and emboss with the same gold powder. Trim the strip to fit on the embossed part. Apply these to the card stock of your choice. Lay a tassel across the strip and add a wax wafer.

Heat the wafer, being careful not to burn the tassel, and then seal. **Hint**: A foil-wrapped piece of cardboard under the card will draw the heat through, and possibly avoid burning the tassel or other embellishments.

Changing Wax Colors

There are a couple of easy ways to change the color of wax. The first is by simply adding two colors of wax together, either by dripping from the stick or by breaking the wafers into smaller chips and combining them. Or you can try this alternative method.

1 When the wax is melted, pour embossing powder over it and reheat it.

2 Put your sealer in the wax. Wait at least thirty seconds and then remove. This technique can really achieve some wonderful results. You can drastically change the color and texture of the wax with embossing powder.

3 Trim this piece into a border strip to be placed on another card.

Here's a great card. Stamp a random pattern all over a border-size strip approximately 5½″ × 3″ (14cm × 7.6cm). Apply this strip to a notecard and trim if necessary. Here I have used a ribbon applied to the card with a bit of wax as an embellishment. I placed wax at the top and heated it. When the wax was warm, I poured on a bit of Chameleon EP, heated it again and sealed it.

Beaded Border

Building on what we've done already, here is a card that combines several techniques. Start with a black postcard-size piece of corrugated board. Rub a bit of embossing fluid down one side. Pour on your favorite powder and then add three more layers of powder, as in chapter one. Here I've used Galaxy EP. Let the piece cool.

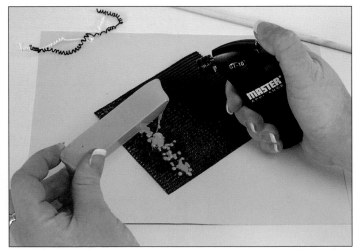

1 Off to the side, prepare some paper cords to put into the wax by twirling them tightly around a paper clip. These cords can be unfurled and recurled several times.

2 Get out a wax stick in a coordinating color and fire up the barbecue lighter. Begin dripping wax on top of the embossed section. Drip enough wax so that it looks like little mountains.

3 Sprinkle on some gold glass beads. Heat the whole piece again if necessary, pour on Amazing Glaze and reheat the whole piece.

4 With the wax still warm, lay the paper cords carefully into the mixture and hold them down with a chopstick.

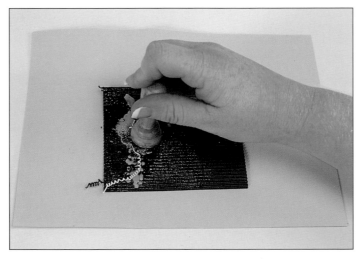

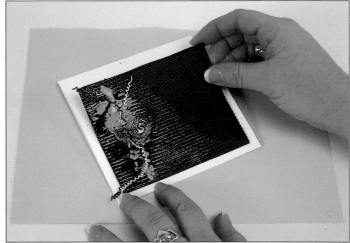

5 Wait thirty seconds for the mixture to cool and press a sealer into a section of the wax. When the piece is cool, color the top of the impression with a silver paint pen.

6 Attach the piece to a notecard with double-stick tape. **Hint**: Remember that double-stick tape holds better than any glue—especially on corrugated papers.

Beadwork Basics

1 When gluing on glass beads, I like to pour them into a resealable plastic bag. I can carefully put the card with the glue on it inside the bag and roll the beads over the card while it is in the bag. For other small jobs like the card with the wax, I just sprinkle the beads on by hand in small amounts.

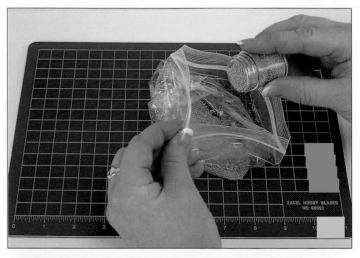

2 On these cards, beads are a simply beautiful accent. The card with the shell has glass beads glued in the grooves of the corrugated board. With the same glue pen, I have squiggled on a border motif.

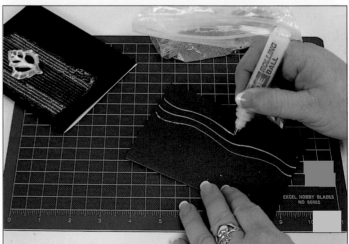

3 Put the card into the bag of beads.

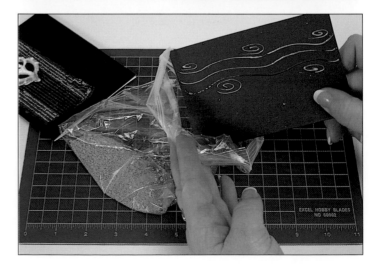

4 Maneuver the beads over the glue.

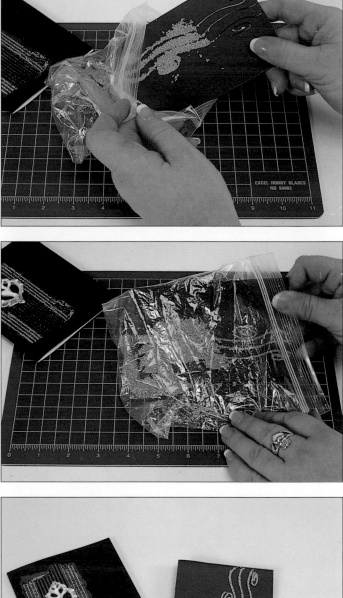

5 Shake off the excess.

6 Allow the cards to set for at least twenty minutes. These are just a few of the many applications you will find for these small wonders—and they come in many colors. Try placing beads in glue swirled over a card in a random pattern, pouring beads on a just-embossed image or sprinkling beads on a just-stamped wax seal.

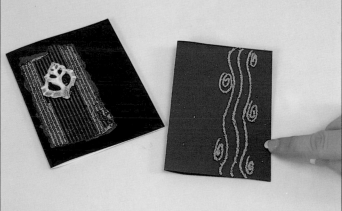

Heartstrings Card

1 Here is a speedy card everyone can master. Start by stamping a pattern all over the front of a card in three different colors. Next (shown on white paper so you can see), about an inch down from the top of the card, near the center, make two small slits, about ½" (12mm) in length, parallel to each other with at least ¼" (6mm) between the slits. Repeat the process at about ¾" (19mm) above the bottom of the card, parallel to the previous cuts.

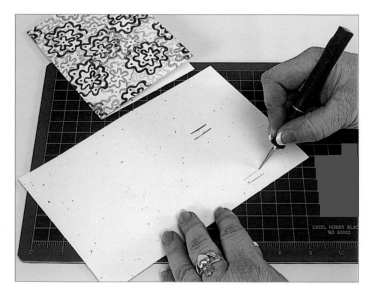

2 Fold two paper cords in half and insert the folded ends into the slits at the top of the card.

3 Take the ends of the cords and insert them into the bottom slits.

4 Trim the excess cord. On this card, a fun variation is to trim a ½" (12mm) strip off the front of the card and add a stained and stamped vellum insert. You could also add swirls of glue and pour on glass beads.

Ideas for Embellishment

(top) **Mayan Hand**: *On torn tan cardstock, emboss the hand in Black Opal. Glue beads into grooves of black corrugated. Allow to dry completely. Tear the corrugated, edge with gold pigment ink and emboss with gold powder. Lay the hand onto the corrugated, and drip black wax over the edges of the piece to adhere. Layer onto a light cardstock.*

(right) **For the Birds**: *Stamp birds in black dye ink on gray graffiti cardstock. Layer on light blue notecard. Break a wax wafer into pieces. Put a small chip in the center of the border and heat. While warm, lay the ribbon into the wax. Use remaining wax on top of the ribbon. Heat and sprinkle with Lapis Lazuli powder. Press in wax sealer.*

(top right) **Snail's Pace:** *In dye or permanent ink, stamp the snail border, then color in with pencils. Trim and add to the notecard accent with foil tape and a wax seal stamped in copper ink.*

(middle left) **Deco Borders:** *Emboss and color two border strips. Add metallic accents to the back border with oil-based paint markers in silver and gold. Punch several small holes in each, and weave in paper cords. Layer on light gray notecard.*

(bottom right) **Two-Tone Wax:** *Place one black and one yellow wax wafer on a torn red strip of paper. Heat and stamp with gold-inked sealer. Layer on top of black corrugated.*

Antique It

Antiquing can be a beautiful technique for many of your favorite stamps. By utilizing both pigment- and dye-based inks on uncoated card stock, adding torn bits of plain paper or buffing the same inks over stamped images within a frame, you can achieve a truly antique finish. I like to use this technique on cards to tone down an overwhelming color combination, or when I feel there is too much white.

The best thing about this method is that you probably have everything you need to begin already—if you've been stamping for a while. Begin with ochre and brown dye-based inks and then add gold and copper pigment-based inks to the piece. Once you have tried this combination, there are several others that work very well. Let's start with the fundamental technique.

Antique Technique

This is a method of burnishing uncoated papers with a metallic finish. It looks especially nice on renaissance images or old clip-art-style designs. Begin by stamping with a black dye or permanent ink stamp pad on smooth uncoated stock (UltraRS paper is perfect for this technique). Let that dry for a minute, and you're ready to begin.

1 Take out your gold pigment-based ink, put your finger in the ink until your finger has plenty of ink on it, and then rub the ink in a circular motion all over the stamped image. You may use a cosmetic sponge instead—but fingers work best.

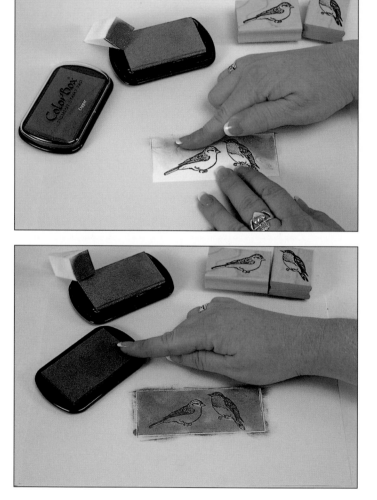

2 Try to get an even coating of the ink over the entire image. You have several options—you could, for example, take copper pigment-based ink and burnish that over the gold for a slightly warmer look.

3 Another possibility is to tap the black, brown or rust dye pad lightly around the edges and buff that extra color in.

4 If you want a burnt-looking edge, cut or tear it around the stamped image, and then use a black dye pad to darken the edge of the paper. Play with this technique: Try different colors under the gold or copper (plum and gold look very nice). Try crumpling the paper after the effect has been achieved for a completely antique look.

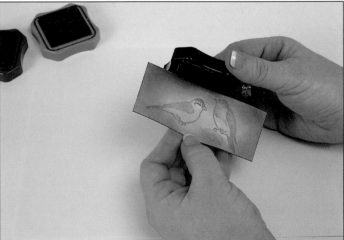

Window to the World

Begin this card by stamping a design in plum, ochre and black dye-based ink on an UltraRS (uncoated) postcard. Antique the card by rubbing gold pigment-based ink evenly over the front with your finger. Set that aside to dry completely. Take a piece of corrugated board 8½″ × 11″ (21.6cm × 27.9cm) and fold it in half lengthwise. Trim it to fit in a business-size envelope. Cut out a window in the card. Attach your antique piece by gluing or taping it to the inside of the card. Tape a used postage stamp or a "postoid" you've made yourself to a piece of red card stock. Trim it so that you leave an ⅛″ (3mm) border around the postage stamp, and tape that piece to the antique piece. Add a tassel or raffia.

Ancient Urn

On a 4½" (11.4cm) square uncoated card, stamp a random pattern with a bold design in black ink. Start the antiquating process by rubbing an ochre dye pad lightly over the card. Add a rust tone dye-based ink around the edge, working toward the center. Begin adding the pigment-based ink layers in gold and then copper, trying to keep the amount of ink as even as possible. Finish this part by lightly adding black dye-based ink over the whole card. Tape a postage stamp to a piece of black corrugated paper lined with gold ink and add that piece to the antique section. After washing your hands, adhere the entire piece to a clean white notecard. **Hint**: We have been using corrugated paper quite often in the past chapters. It is fun to note that paper cords fit in the grooves, as well as in the cut ends, of corrugated cardboard.

Angel Flight

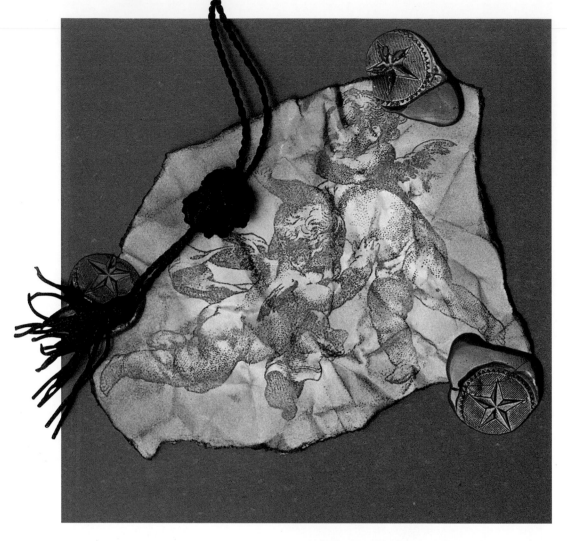

1 Stamp angels in black dye-based ink on light-weight white uncoated paper. Add brown tones to the piece with ochre, brown and rust dye-based inks. Antique with gold and copper pigment-based ink.

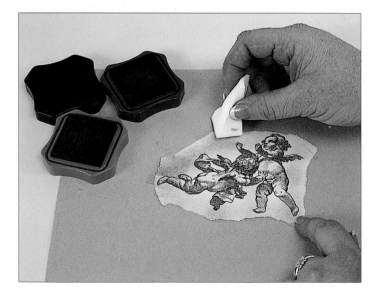

2 Tear the edges of the paper and crumple it. Lightly touch the cracks and crevices with a black dye pad.

3 Attach the paper to the front of a notecard with wax, pressing the hot wax with a coordinating seal.

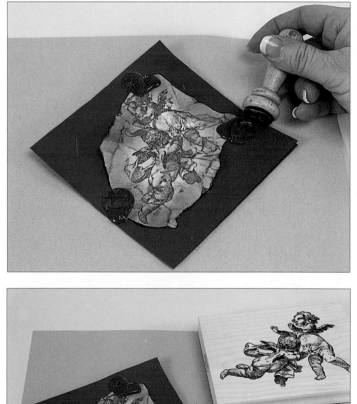

Enhance Old Pieces

You can antique pieces that you have already colored, like this teapot.

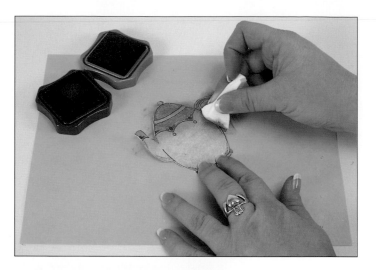

More Antique Ideas

(top right) Stamp the music sheet in black dye ink on lightweight paper. Antique the gold and copper pigment inks. Tear the edges, and attach with wax to a notecard. Add tassels to finish.

(bottom left) **Antique Postage:** Stamp postage triangle in black dye ink. Mask and stamp in moon face. Antique as directed. Cut out and layer into black wax. Add border of corrugated dyed with green ink. Finish with a tassel.

Paper Metallic

If you are looking for something unique to try with your stamps, this is the technique for you. With water-based metallic markers and oil-based paint markers you can invent some lovely papers that have the appearance of soft brushed metals. The water-based markers can be used directly on bold stamps, mixed with water, buffed on with a sponge or with your fingers, applied to wax or embossed images and even added between layers of super-embossed pieces. Oil-based markers are more limited in function but are better for some applications, like writing on dark papers. These markers can also be used on wax, and are especially good for outlining images. If you can't find these types of pens, try using interference inks or paints to mimic the effects. These paints and inks have a metallic or pearlized quality and can be applied with sponges or brushes.

The Soft Metal Finish

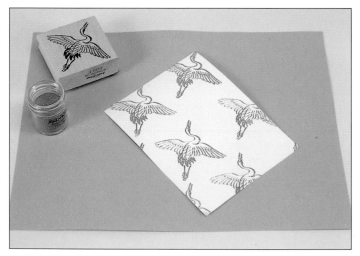

1 On a standard-size postcard, stamp and emboss a random pattern in silver. Let cool.

2 Take a blue metallic water-based pen and blot out some of the paint onto a paint tray. Apply the paint in streaks across the card, and buff the paint into the paper with your finger or a cosmetic sponge.

3 Repeat step two using a purple marker. Be sure to completely cover the embossed images. Allow the paint to dry thoroughly. This is important, because this paint does not look metallic until it is dry.

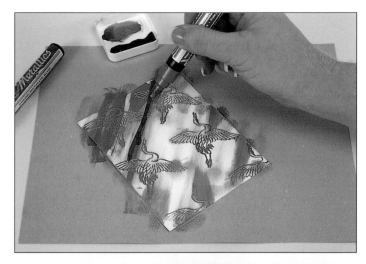

4 When the paint is thoroughly dry, emboss a few more images in silver over the top of the postcard.

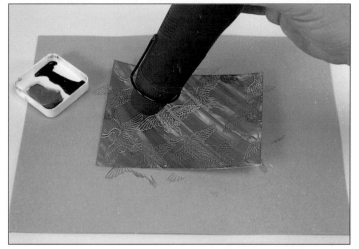

5 Affix the postcard to a square notecard. If you wish, emboss the same image on the plain border, or add a paper cord or a tassel for emphasis.

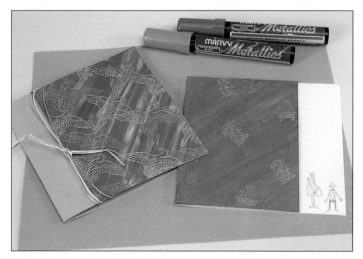

Surprise Package

1 Color a plain white piece of card stock with a pink metallic water-based marker.

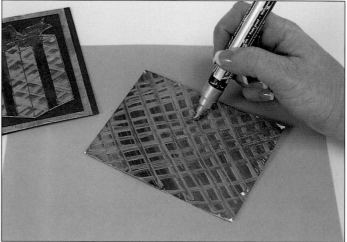

2 Draw lines with a green marker to make a plaid pattern.

3 Soften the line with a sponge.

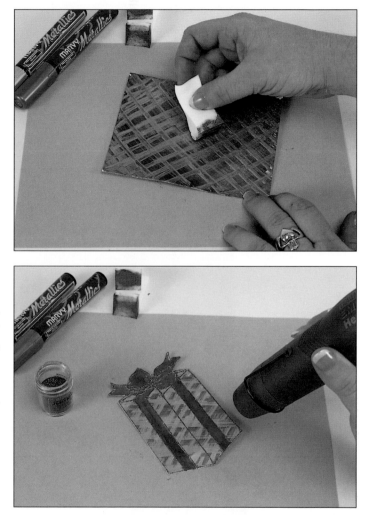

4 Once the piece is completely dry, emboss the package with a complementary color darker than the metallic ink. Color over the bow section with the same pink pen. Now cut out the package and set it aside. Dab out some of the paint from the pens onto a paint tray and, on a postcard-size piece of vellum, use a fan brush to apply the paint in quick strokes. When all pieces are dry, layer the vellum onto purple card stock. Adhere the cut out package to a purple piece of card stock cut to reveal a ¼" (6mm) of vellum.

Kimono Swirls

On a light brown deckle postcard, emboss a swirl stamp in Egyptian Gold EP. Line the insides of the swirls with a silver oil-based paint pen. Now stamp the kimono stamp and emboss it with Malachite EP. Color it in with water-based pens, and then accent the flowers with the silver marker. Finish the kimono by outlining the edge with the silver marker. Cut it out and tape it to the deckle postcard. Apply the postcard to a purple notecard.

Rustic Seal

1 Try this with one of the super-embossed pieces you've done. Add some blobs of gold paint marker (I have used an oil-based one) to the cooled surface.

2 Reheat a small section of the embossed piece, and apply a tiny amount of embossing fluid to your seal.

3 Embed the seal into the hot EP.

4 When the seal has cooled, take a gold paint pen and color the raised parts of the seal. **Hint**: Both types of pens work on embossed pieces and on wax. The water-based type looks exceptionally good between layers of glazes. You can see this on the next card.

Elegance in Black

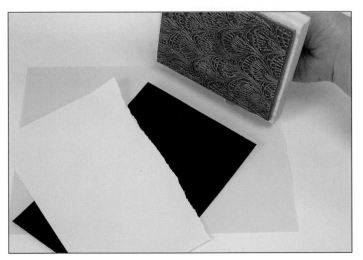

1 Begin by masking off a diagonal section of the front of a glossy black notecard.

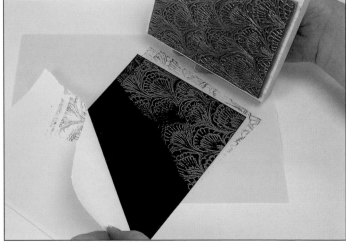

2 Stamp with a giant background coated in copper pigment-based ink. Now emboss it, being careful not to handle the glossy paper too much. Every little mark shows! **Hint**: Use a clean sheet of folded bond paper to cover the card while handling it.

3 When the piece has cooled, put your mask back in place and begin lightly smearing the metallic paint over the embossed image with your fingers, a sponge or a paper towel.

4 Add a second color for a nice touch.

5 Pull the mask away slowly; allow the card to dry.

6 Add a wax seal to the card.

7 Accent the wax with paint markers to finish the card. **Hint**: Do not use embossing powders with glitter on techniques that require rubbing over the surface. They are too textured for the paint to adhere.

Jazz It Up

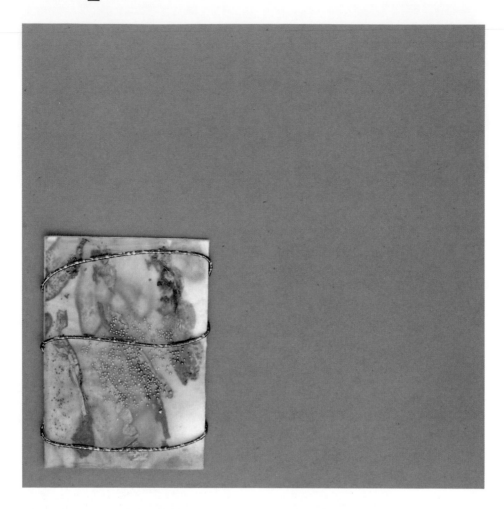

1 Here is an interesting idea for another super-embossed piece. Take a piece you've embossed at least twice and scribble water-based metallic markers over the surface.

2 Reheat the surface, and then add another layer of clear or Amazing Glaze. The scribbles look like foil floating in between the layers.

3 Sprinkle on a few beads and another layer of glaze.

4 Reheat the piece and attach it to a notecard.

More Paper Metallic Ideas

(top left) **Collage Mr. Sun:** *Using a torn metallic background as a base, emboss Mr. Sun in a metallic color powder. Layer this piece to a handmade paper placed diagonally across a notecard. Trim the excess and add raffia for the final touch.*

(top right) **Moon and Star Card:** *This is a quick card to put together once you've made up several metallic backgrounds. Emboss the stars and moons over a metallic marker base. Add dots and outline the stars and moon with a fine metallic marker.*

(bottom right) **Lovely Kimono:** *Layer this cut-out kimono on several pieces colored with metallic marker. The crane part was made by embossing and then rubbing the metallic ink over the cooled surface with a paper towel.*

(top) **Fleur-de-Lis:** *Stamp and use bronze embossing powder over the images on a piece of smooth card stock. With a piece of cosmetic sponge spread the metallic ink evenly over the entire piece.*

(bottom) **Wild Metals:** *This card was created with pieces of card stock brayered with waterbased metallic markers. Simply apply the ink directly to a rubber brayer and roll it across a stamped paper.*

CHAPTER 8

Handmade Ornaments

Most people who do crafts have played with some sort of clay. Here is the chance to take the knowledge you've gained and incorporate it into a new experience. Most of these clays are easy to use, but they do have a few requirements. Poly clays need special equipment for molding and baking. You don't want to use anything from the kitchen with these clays, including cookie sheets. When I bake these pieces of clay, I put them on cut-up brown paper bags so I can throw the bags away.

Paper clays are a bit easier to deal with in some ways because they are lighter weight, can be air dried and can be colored with pens or colored pencils, just like paper. Both of these types of clays can be used to create beads and beautiful ornaments for cards.

River Rock Fossil Card

Begin with a stone-colored poly clay. Make stone color yourself by adding Antique Lead embossing powder to a small chunk of white clay. Mix the color well by kneading the powder into the clay. I use a quarter teaspoon of powder to one ounce of clay.

1 Roll out a marble-size ball of clay.

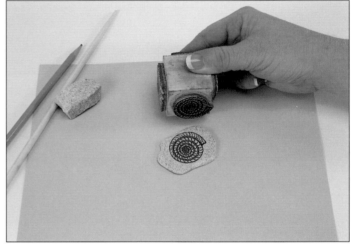

2 Ink a shell stamp with black dye-based ink, and stamp the flattened shape.

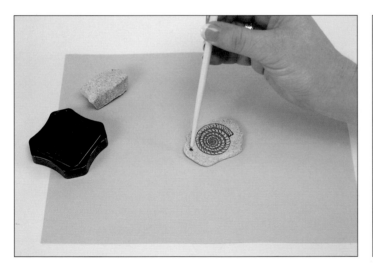

3 Create a hole to tie the stone onto your card. Bake as directed. I attached this piece to my card with paper cords.

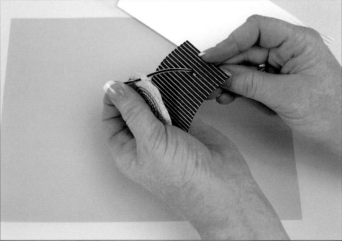

Little Buddha Card

Start with plain white poly clay. Mold the clay into a stone-like shape. Ink the Buddha stamp with dye-based ink, stamp and bake. After the stone has cooled, color it by rubbing dye-based inks into it with a paper towel. Be careful not to get the ink too dark: It will overshadow the stamp image. Apply the stone to an embossed card with an all-over pattern. Wrap the stone with paper cords and trim. **Hint**: Look around at garage sale or thrift stores for an old toaster oven and other kitchen equipment to use for poly clays and other craft projects (like shrink plastic) that require baking plastics.

Celtic Stone Card

Begin by making a stone shape with poly clay. Imprint a clean stamp into the clay, and then bake the piece. When the clay has cooled, rub black dye-based ink into the lettering. Take a water-based metallic gold pen and color the top of the stone. When it is completely dry, attach the stone to corrugated board, and then layer it onto the card. **Hint**: Remember that whenever you add more than ¼" (6mm) in thickness to a card, you will need extra postage.

Swirly Bead Card

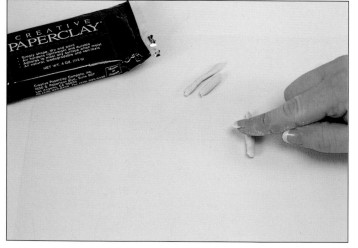

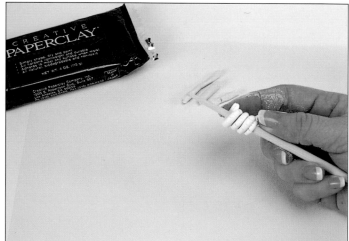

MAKING BEADS

To make the beads on this card, begin with a narrow chopstick, a skewer or a toothpick. Roll a small amount of paper clay into a worm shape and wrap it around the toothpick. Pull it off carefully and allow it to air dry. You'll be able to make several beads in a matter of minutes, so make plenty for future use.

Color only the ones you'll use for this card, because they can be colored at any time. I colored these with water-based metallic markers and rolled two of them in bronze pigment-based ink. Add the beads to a border card stamped with pigment-based inks by hanging them from paper cords knotted together.

More Ornament Ideas

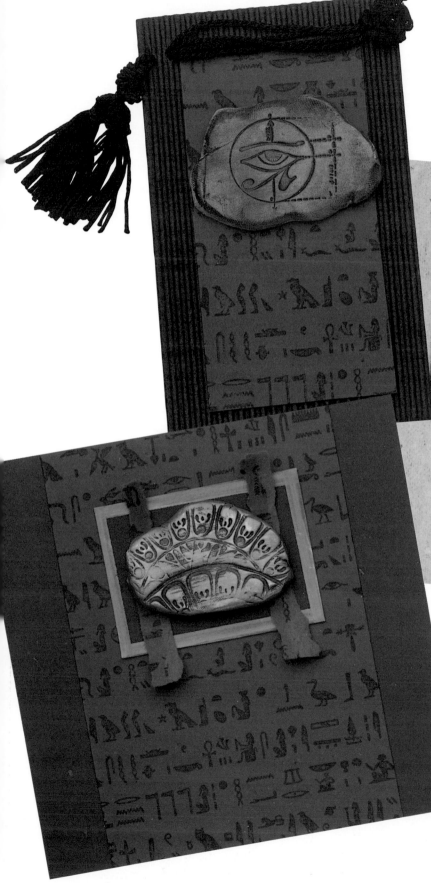

(top left) **Stone Eye:** *Do not add any metallic ink on this clay stone—just a bit of dye ink in a dark color.*

(middle right) **Easy Beads:** *Create teardrop-shaped beads with clay, and stamp with small images. Be sure to add holes to the beads before baking. After baking apply two tones of ink, and accent with markers. Hang the beads with papercords. Add layers underneath for interest.*

(bottom left) **Stone of Egypt:** *Begin by stamping and backing a rock-shaped piece of clay. Let cool. Rub with a black dye pad, and let dry. Lightly coat with copper metallic marker. Apply to a stamped card.*

CHAPTER

Brayers & Bleach

Never underestimate the brayer as a creative tool. With some tube watercolors and the brayer, you can create beautiful cards to stamp on. Bleach can also be used to give your creations unique effects. We'll start out with the basics.

Wild Brayer Backgrounds

Ideas to use for making great cards with brayers include using texturing techniques, sealing layers together, and applying watercolor paints and bleach. Brayers are not just a tool for a technique or two—you should keep them out and use them often. There are many types of brayers available. Start with a basic rubber brayer. Even if it is only used for gluing purposes, a brayer is a necessary item for every stamper.

SEALING GLUED LAYERS WITH THE BRAYER

A brayer is a great tool for creating a complete seal between two pieces of paper, especially if you are covering cardboard for small books or doing a collage-style card. Begin by applying a light film of glue to one side of each layer to be glued together. Layer the pieces together. When you have the pieces positioned, take a clean brayer and roll it over the layers. The brayer creates a tight seal with no air bubbles. If you like to use rubber cement as your adhesive, be sure to wait until the pieces have dried before you begin the layering process.

Watercolor and Your Brayer

By utilizing watercolors straight from the tube, you can create some vivid artistic backgrounds to stamp on. The technique is really quite simple and only requires a few supplies: inexpensive watercolors in the tube, plastic trays or paper plates, paper and a brayer.

1 Begin by squeezing small amounts of several colors of paint onto your plate or tray.

2 Wet your brayer lightly, and roll it over the colors on the plate a few times. Don't overmix the colors on the plate on your first run.

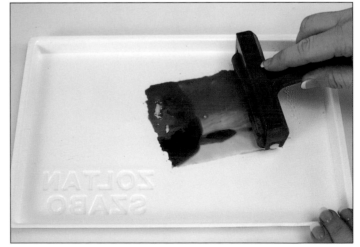

3 Blend the colors on the paper you have chosen. Since the paint will dry through evaporation, you can use it on most types of paper, including coated stocks. Set the piece aside to dry.

4 While a piece is still wet, add blotches of ink from your markers (any type).

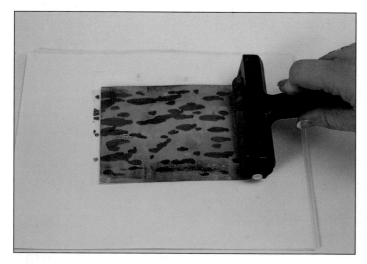

5 Brayer the piece again.

The possibilities are endless—make an afternoon of it! Save all the parts you make for a card-making day. **Hint**: For an elegant touch, try applying a small amount of powdered metallic pigment and brayer it into the wet paint. Seal the finished piece with a light spray fixative after you stamp the piece.

Watercolor Masterpiece Cards

When the piece is dry, you can apply stamped images in a variety of ways. Pigment-based inks will work, but the usual rules are still true—if you have used a coated stock underneath, you still should emboss. Dye-based inks will give you a soft look. I prefer permanent inks for a beautiful black on these brilliant backgrounds. Try all three types of inks to see the differences.

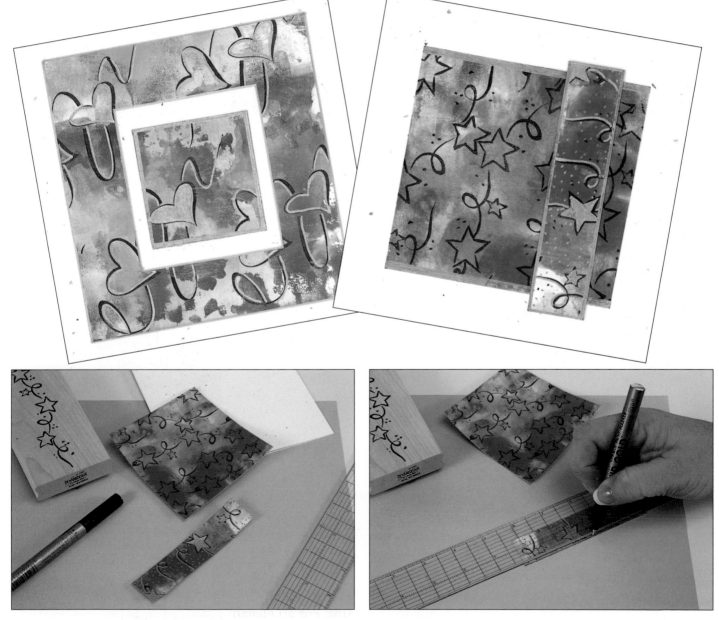

1 I stamped these pieces with flowing designs in permanent black ink. (Remember, you must work quickly with permanent inks.) After trimming a 1″ (2.5cm) strip of the card off, I then trimmed that strip with a gold paint pen and colored in a few stars.

2 The remaining large square was adhered to a fresh white card with double-stick tape.

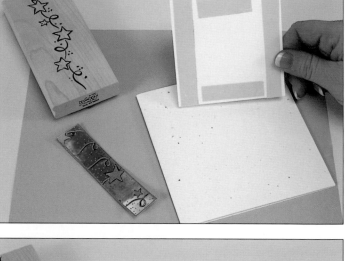

3 The border strip was taped to the front of the card. Playing with paints and inks together will give you a better understanding of what each can do, which will in turn broaden your creativity.

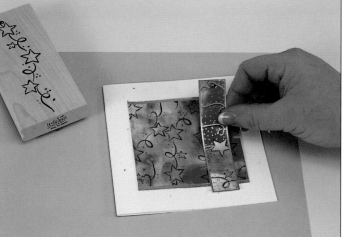

Using Bleach

Something I know you have around the house that is great for stamping is bleach. No, it won't hurt your stamps—just wipe your stamps well with water (no chemical cleaners, just water) afterward. This technique will give you varied results on different papers, so test out a variety of colors before finalizing your decisions.

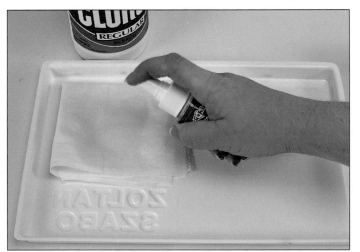

1 Begin by creating a pad out of paper towels, and then pour on a bit of bleach. I put the bleach in a spritzer bottle for more control, so I can just spritz on a bit more when needed. Put your stamp to the makeshift pad.

2 Stamp the image on a dark uncoated paper. Now wait as the image appears. This can be used as a background for many cards.

Bubble Wrap Trick

1 Another trick to try with your brayer is to brayer color onto textured items like bubble wrap. Here I have inked the bubble wrap with dye-based inks.

2 Run the brayer across the wrap.

3 Brayer that texture on your favorite white or light-colored paper.

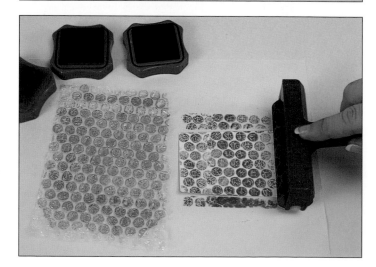

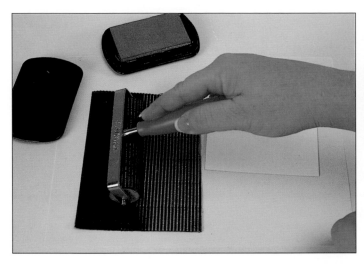 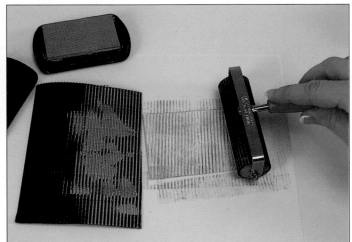

Try the same trick on corrugated board with pigment-based inks. Dye-based inks dry too fast on this board because it is so porous.

 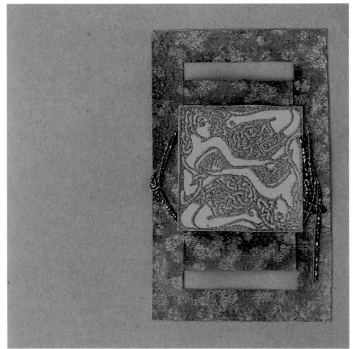

Simply Delicious Deco Card

1 Put straight bleach in a small spritzer bottle. Spray bleach across the front of a cinnamon-colored card; spraying along only one side gives an airbrush effect as the bleach evaporates. Let the paper dry completely.

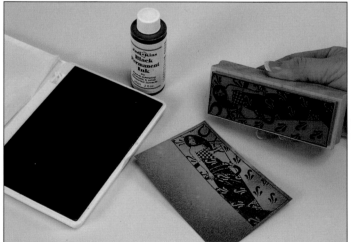

2 Stamp the lady in permanent ink along the right-hand side of the card. Trim the piece down to 4" × 5" (10.2cm × 12.7cm).

3 Embellish the image with a gold paint marker.

4 Layer the piece to another cinnamon notecard. **Hint**: Try spraying several different colors of paper. Come back the next day to stamp or emboss. You'll get a true final color by waiting.

Gallery

Coffee, tea or me?

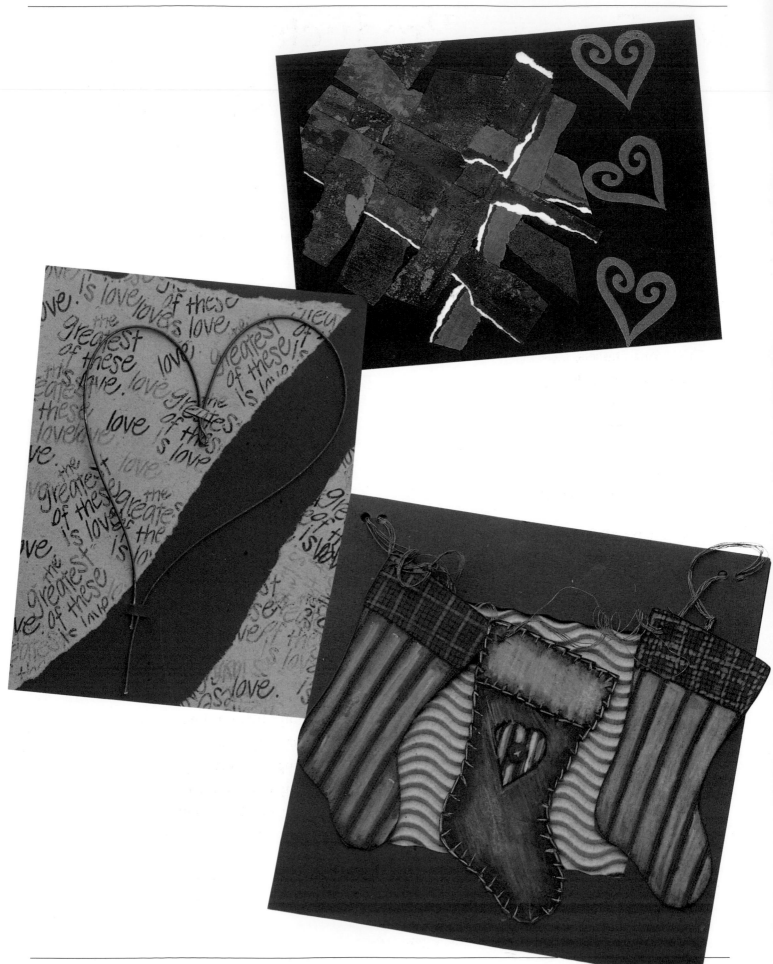

My Favorite Products

Listed here are some of the stamping items I enjoy using:

Papers by JudiKins

C-Thru ruler

Speedball detachable brayer

Embossing powders from JudiKins, Draggin' Ink, Viva Las Vegastamps

Amazing Glaze from JudiKins

Permanent ink from JudiKins

Pigment inks from Colorbox

Dye inks from Marvy

Paper cords, tassels, glass beads from JudiKins

Sailor glue for beads

Wax wafers from JudiKins

Watercolors from Yasutomo

STAMPS

Here is a listing of the stamps used in this book by page number:

14 sun, people and middle graphics by A Stamp in the Hand; top right graphic and heart by Stampacadabra; two-heart stamp by De Nami; sprinkle stamp by Viva Las Vegastamps; cat by Ruby Red Rubber

15 left three borders by A Stamp in the Hand; right border by Magenta; snail by Hot Potatoes; top right leaf by Rubber Monger; flower-and-insect stamp by Claudia Rose; turtle by Hot Potatoes; flower by Love You to Bits; middle leaf by Carmen's Veranda; birdhouse by Carmen's Veranda; beetle by Coffee Break

16 teacup by Art Gone Wild; pirate boy by Coffee Break; standing angel by Carmen's Veranda; boy by Viva Las Vegastamps; deco angel by Zettiology; flower bouquet by Judi-Kins; world by Toybox; woodcut by Rubber Monger; circular flowers by JudiKins

17 left child and fish stamps by Curtis Uyeda; top right Asian stamp by Zettiology; Asian boy by Stampacadabra; Celtic knot, Egyp-tian and Aztec stamps by JudiKins; alligator by Stampacadabra; wax seals by JudiKins

26 circle design by Ruby Red Rubber sun by Stampacadabra

27 feather by JudiKins heart by Carmen's Veranda

28-33 stamps by JudiKins

36-38 stamps by JudiKins

39 border stamp by Magenta

40-47 stamps by JudiKins

48-49 stamps by Carmen's Veranda

52-55 stamps by JudiKins

61 wax seals by JudiKins

63-65 wax seals by JudiKins

68-69 stamps by JudiKins

70 hand by JudiKins birds by Carmen's Veranda

71 wax seals and deco swirl stamp by JudiKins snail border by Magenta

76 stamps by Viva Las Vegastamps

77 stamps by Hot Potatoes

78-79 stamps and wax seals by JudiKins

80 stamps by Art Gone Wild

81 stamps and wax seals by JudiKins

84-85 stamps by JudiKins

86-87 stamps by Art Gone Wild

88-90 stamps by JudiKins

91-93 stamps and wax seals by JudiKins

96-97 stamps by JudiKins

100-101 stamps by JudiKins

102 stamps by Curtis Uyeda

103 stamps by JudiKins

104 stamps by Hot Potatoes

105 stamps by JudiKins

111-112 stamps by De Nami

113, 115 stamps by JudiKins

116-117 stamps by Magenta

My Favorite Products **123**

Stamp Companies and Publications

Alice in Rubberland
P.O. Box 9262
Seattle, WA 98109

Art Gone Wild
3110 Payne Ave.
Cleveland, OH 44114
Phone: (800) 945-3980
Fax: (216) 241-1479
E-mail: artgwild@aol.com

A Stamp In the Hand
20630 S. Leapwood Ave.
Suite B
Carson, CA 90746
Phone: (310) 329-8555

Claudia Rose
15 Baumgarten Rd.
Saugerties, NY 12477
Phone/Fax: (914) 679-9235

Carmen's Veranda
P.O. Box 1539
Placentia, CA 92871
Phone: (888) 227-6367
Web address:
www.carmensveranda.com

Coffee Break Designs
P.O. Box 34281
Indianapolis, IN 46234

Curtis Uyeda
3326 St. Michael Dr.
Palo Alto, CA 94306

DeNami Design
P.O. Box 5617
Kent, WA 98064
Phone: (253) 639-2546

Draggin' Ink
P.O. Box 24135
Santa Barbara, CA 93121

Hot Potatoes
209 Tenth Ave., Suite 311
Nashville, TN 37203
Phone: (615) 255-4055
Fax: (615) 255-4556

JudiKins
17832 S. Hobart Blvd.
Gardena, CA 90248
Phone: (310) 515-1115
Fax: (310) 323-6619

Love You to Bits
P.O. Box 5748
Redwood City, CA 94063
Phone: (800) 546-LYTB/(800)
546-5982

Magenta
351 Blain
Mont-Saint-Hilaire
Quebec, Canada J3H3B4
Phone: (514) 446-5253
Fax: (514) 464-6353

Moe Wubba
P.O. Box 1445, Dept. B
San Luis Obispo, CA 93406
Phone: (805) 547-1MOE/(805)
547-1663

Museum of Modern Rubber
3015 Glendale Blvd.
Suite 100C
Los Angeles CA 90039
Phone: (213) 662-1133

Paper Parachute
P.O. Box 91385
Portland, OR 97291-0385

Ruby Red Rubber
P.O. Box 2076
Yorba Linda, CA 92686
Phone: (714) 970-7584

Rubber Baby Buggy Bumpers
1331 W. Mountain Ave.
Fort Collins, CO 80521
Phone: (970) 224-3499

Rubber Monger
P.O. Box 435
Moorpark, CA 93020-0435
Fax: (888) 9 MONGER/(888)
966-6437

Rubbermoon
P.O. Box 3258
Hayden Lake, ID 83835

Stampacadabra
5091 N. Fresno St., Suite 133
Fresno, CA 93710
Phone: (209) 227-7247
Fax: (209) 229-2642

Stampscapes
7451 Warner Ave., #E124
Huntington Beach, CA 92647

Stamps Happen, Inc.
369 S. Acacia Ave.
Fullerton, CA 92631
Phone: (714) 879-9894

Stamp Oasis
4750 W. Sahara Ave., Suite 17
Las Vegas, NV 89102
Phone: (800) 234-8735

Toybox Rubber Stamps
P.O. Box 1487
Healdsburg, CA 95448
Phone: (707) 431-1400
Fax: (707) 431-2048

Twenty Two Teeth
6167 N. Broadway, No. 322
Chicago, IL 60660

Viva Las Vegastamps
1008 E. Sahara Ave.
Las Vegas, NV 89104
Phone: (702) 836-9118

Wizard of Ah's Stamps
4538 W. Lord Redman Loop
Tucson, AZ 85741

Worth Repeating
227 N. East St.
New Auburn, WI 54757
Phone: (715) 237-2011

Zettiology
P.O. Box 5681
Bellevue, WA 98006

For more information on stamping
or stamp stores in your area, try
these stamping publications:

National Stampagraphic
P.O. Box 370985
Las Vegas, NV 89137-0985
Phone/Fax: (702) 233-4757

The Rubberstamper
225 Gordons Corner Road
P.O. Box 420
Manalapan, NJ 07726-0420
Phone: (800) 969-7176

RUBBERSTAMPMADNESS
408 S.W. Monroe, #210
Corvallis, OR 97330
Phone: (541) 752-0075

Stamper's Sampler &
Somerset Studio
22992 Millcreek, Suite B
Laguna Hills, CA
Phone: (714) 380-7318
Fax: (714) 380-9355

Rubberstamp Sourcebook &
Travelers Guide to
Rubberstamping
Cornucopia Press
4739 University Way NE
Suite 1610-A
Seattle, WA 98105
Phone: (206) 528-8120

Vamp Stamp News
P.O. Box 386
Hanover, MD 21076-0386
Phone: (410) 760-3377

Index